From Lehi to Moroni

R. COLTRANE

CFI · AN IMPRINT OF CEDAR FORT, INC. · SPRINGVILLE, UTAH

Dedicated to Anne, Renae, and Rodger

Text © 2018 R. Coltrane
Illustrations © 2018 R. Coltrane

This is not an official publication of The Church of Jesus Christ of Latter-day Saints. The opinions and views expressed herein belong solely to the author and do not necessarily represent the opinions or views of Cedar Fort, Inc. Permission for the use of sources, graphics, and photos is also solely the responsibility of the author.

ISBN 13: 978-1-4621-2264-6

Published by CFI, an imprint of Cedar Fort, Inc.
2373 W. 700 S., Springville, UT 84663
Distributed by Cedar Fort, Inc., www.cedarfort.com

141 8317

   Library of Congress Control Number: 2018946810

Cover design and typesetting by Shawnda T. Craig
Cover design © 2018 Cedar Fort, Inc.
Edited by Kathryn Watkins and Kaitlin Barwick

Printed by Artin Printing Co.
82485
8-13-18

Printed in South Korea

10 9 8 7 6 5 4 3 2 1

Printed on acid-free paper

Contents

Book of Mormon

INTRODUCTION

The Book of Mormon was written by different prophets over hundreds of years, and each prophet wrote thinking about you. Heavenly Father guided each prophet to teach us how to live. Regardless of the differences in our world today, the same ideas of how we should live are the same.

Mormon transferred all of the writings into one set of gold plates, which tells the history of two large civilizations, the Jaredites and the Israelites. The Jaredites arrived in the Americas around the time of the Tower of Babel, when people were cursed to speak different languages. The Israelites came from Jerusalem and eventually split into two groups: the Nephites and the Lamanites.

Mormon's son Moroni finished the plates, added some more revelations, then hid them in the Hill Cumorah. Hundreds of years later, the same Moroni appeared to Joseph Smith as a spirit to show him the location of the buried plates.

Joseph Smith taught that the Book of Mormon was the most correct book on earth. It's the keystone of the religion, and you can get closer to God by following its ideas and teachings than any other book.

As you read the stories in this book, think about how they apply to your life and use these teachings to become closer to God.

Lehi
and
HIS WARNING

(1 NEPHI 1)

Six hundred years before Jesus was born, Jerusalem was a wicked place. God sent prophets to tell the Jews to repent, but the people rejected His prophets and even killed them, causing their own future destruction.

Lehi lived in Jerusalem his whole life. He loved the city and all the people who lived there, but he knew they were wicked. He prayed and begged the Lord to help the people repent. Suddenly, a giant pillar of fire appeared on a rock in front of him. In shock, Lehi ran home and immediately fell on his bed, where he was overcome with the feeling of the Holy Ghost.

Lehi had a vision of God sitting on His throne surrounded by angels. The brightest angel approached Lehi with twelve others following, handing him a book and prompting him to read it. The book said that Jerusalem would be destroyed because of their wickedness. Many people would die, and the rest would be prisoners in Babylon.

When Lehi awoke from the vision, he was afraid for his family and the city of Jerusalem. He immediately ran to tell the people that they had to repent or else they would be destroyed. He also testified that one day a Messiah would come to redeem the world.

The people laughed and made fun of Lehi's visions. They didn't want to repent because they wanted everything to stay the same, and they were angry with Lehi for asking them to change. Just like they had done with the other prophets, the people in Jerusalem planned to kill Lehi, but the Lord had other plans for him.

Lehi
and His
ESCAPE FROM JERUSALEM

(1 NEPHI 2)

One night, the Lord visited Lehi in a dream and warned him that he had to escape the city because he was in danger.

Lehi immediately gathered his family and told them to pack everything they would need for their journey. It was difficult for them all to leave because they walked away from their home, their land, and all of their gold and other precious things.

They loaded everything they would need to survive onto some of their animals and left their lives in Jerusalem behind.

They began their escape by walking into the wilderness. After three exhausting days, they reached the borders of the land, next to the Red Sea. They chose to set up their camp there, because they would have access to water and more of a chance to find food.

Nephi

and

THE BRASS PLATES

(1 NEPHI 2)

Heavenly Father commanded Lehi in a dream that his four sons, Laman, Lemuel, Sam, and Nephi, should go back to Jerusalem and get the brass plates that had a record of their ancestors. The brass plates were in the possession of Laban, a wicked man in the city.

Laman and Lemuel, the eldest, were hesitant. They worried about the journey and how they would get the plates from such a powerful man. Their younger brother Nephi knew that the Lord wouldn't give them a commandment that they couldn't complete. He knew that the Lord would help them to complete their task no matter how difficult it may appear to be. So the four of them left on their journey back to Jerusalem.

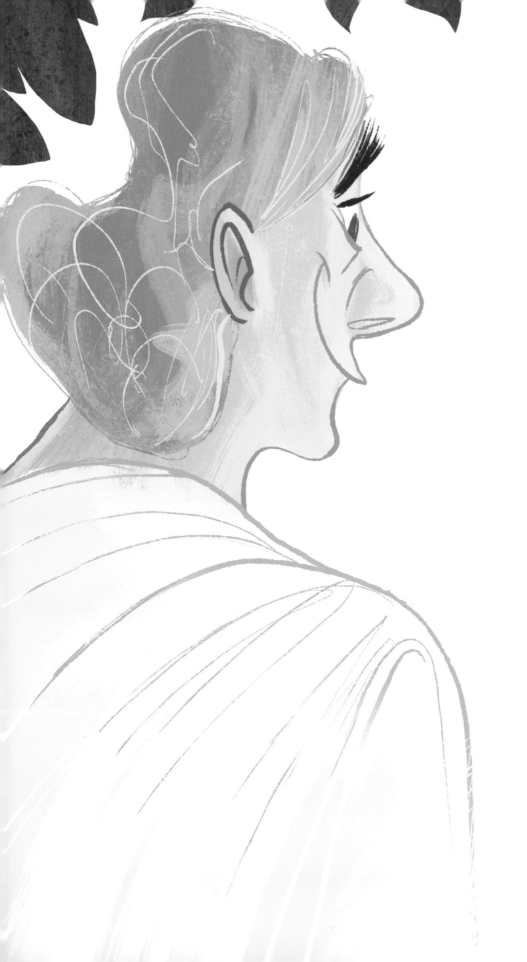

Nephi

and

HIS UNFAITHFUL BROTHERS

(1 NEPHI 3)

When they got to the border of Jerusalem the brothers cast lots, which would be like drawing straws or flipping a coin. It was decided that Laman would go into Laban's house to ask for the plates. Laman was scared and reluctant, but he went in to speak to Laban anyway. When he asked for the plates, Laban became really angry. He accused Laman of being a robber and threatened to kill him.

Laman ran back to his brothers, and after hearing what happened, everyone but Nephi wanted to give up. Nephi wanted to do what the Lord commanded. He had the idea that they should go back to their home, get all of their gold and silver, and trade it to Laban for the plates.

Nephi explained that the plates were important in order to preserve their history for their future descendants.

Laban was excited when he saw all of the gold and silver—he wanted to keep the riches and the plates, so he ordered his guards to kill the four brothers.

Nephi, Laman, Lemuel, and Sam were chased out of Jerusalem by Laban's guards. They escaped by hiding in a cave. Laman and Lemuel were so angry that they started to hit Nephi and Sam with sticks. An angel appeared stopping Laman and Lemuel from hurting their brothers. The angel told them to go back to Laban one last time.

Nephi

AND LABAN

(1 NEPHI 4)

It was dark when Nephi and his brothers arrived back in Jerusalem. Nephi told his brothers to stay outside the city. Nephi crept in alone, unsure of what he was going to do, but filled with faith that the Lord would help him achieve this difficult task.

As he approached Laban's house, there was a man lying on the ground, passed out after drinking too much. As Nephi tiptoed past him, he realized

it was Laban! This was the opportunity he was waiting for. Afraid that Laban would attack him, he slowly removed the sword from Laban's belt. Suddenly, Nephi was prompted by the Holy Ghost to kill Laban. Nephi was confused, he didn't want to break the commandments. But the prompting came again.

The Lord spoke to Nephi through the Holy Ghost telling him that the life of one wicked man would save an entire civilization. Knowing that it was what Lord wanted him to do, Nephi killed Laban, dressed in Laban's clothes, and ran into the house to get the brass plates.

As Nephi was looking for the plates, he met a servant called Zoram who knew how to get the plates. Nephi ordered Zoram to fetch and bring the brass plates to the outskirts of the city. Zoram obeyed, fooled by Nephi's disguise.

When Laman, Lemuel, and Sam saw Laban and his servant coming toward them, they ran away because they were afraid that Nephi had been killed. Nephi took off his disguise and called after his brothers. When they saw that he was alive, they were relieved. Zoram was then afraid of the strangers, but Nephi assured him that he could be free if he came with them into the wilderness.

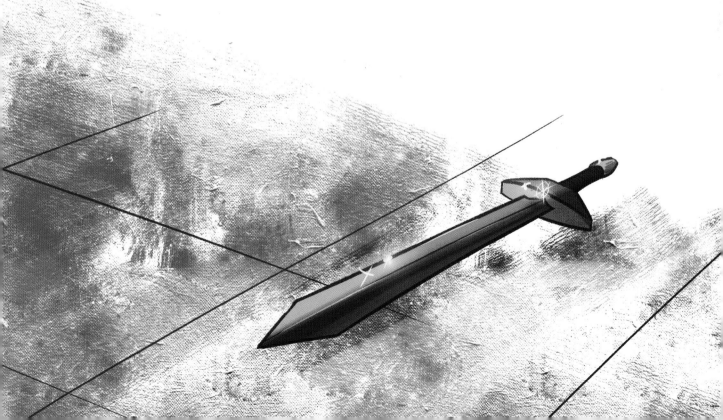

Lehi and THE LIAHONA

(1 NEPHI 7, 16)

Not long after his sons returned safely, Lehi had a vision instructing him to send his four sons back to Jerusalem, again. Their mission was to ask Lehi's friend Ishmael to join them in the wilderness.

When Nephi and his brothers explained everything Lehi had seen, Ishmael immediately gathered his wife, sons, and daughters and told them to pack their provisions and animals.

Ishmael and his family embarked on the difficult journey toward Lehi's camp. After returning safely, Laman, Lemuel, Nephi, Sam and Zoram each married one of Ishmael's daughters.

Now that the group was complete, Lehi was prompted to lead the large group further into the wilderness. He found a metal ball outside of his tent, which he called the Liahona, it acted like a compass and showed Lehi and his family where the Lord wanted them to go.

After days of traveling everyone was exhausted, miserable, and hungry. Laman, Lemuel, and Nephi tried to hunt food for the family, but Nephi's bow broke, and Laman and Lemuel's bows lost their strength. The journey

continued, and Ishmael died. His children were distraught, blaming Lehi for their suffering, hunger, and tiredness.

Laman, Lemuel, and the children of Ishmael were very angry at Lehi and the Lord because they had no food. Nephi warned them that they were being unfaithful, which upset Laman and Lemuel because their younger brother was trying to teach them. They made a plan to kill Nephi, but the voice of the Lord punished them and told them to repent. They repented, and the Lord blessed the family with food.

Lehi
and
HIS WONDERFUL DREAM

(1 NEPHI 8)

One night, Lehi had an incredibly powerful dream. Using the Holy Ghost, Lehi understood that the dream meant so much more than it seemed to be.

The dream began with Lehi wandering in a dark, sad wasteland for hours. Feeling hopeless, Lehi prayed. When he opened his eyes , he saw a tree, filled with fruit, glowing in the distance. He quickly made his way to the tree and ate the fruit, which was the most delicious thing he had ever tasted. He felt happy and blessed. Lehi searched for his family and saw them next to a river. Lehi's wife, Sariah, and Sam and Nephi made their way to Lehi, but Laman and Lemuel stayed by the river, refusing to move.

Thousands of people tried to make their way to the tree by following a straight, narrow path holding on to a rod of iron. Many of them would wander off, falling in to the river, getting lost in the darkness, or choosing to join the sinful people who were all in a huge building on the other side of the river. The sinful people boasted about their possessions and laughed at the people trying to get to the tree.

Those who did make it to the tree were overcome with happiness and excitement to have made their journey through the difficult conditions.

The Holy Ghost told Lehi that the tree represented the love of God, which meant that the delicious fruit could only be eaten by those who were righteous and accepted Jesus's sacrifice.

The iron rod and the straight and narrow path are a symbols of the gospel of Jesus Christ, which gave people a guide to cling to and pointed them in

the right direction. When people let go of the gospel, stop believing, or break commandments, they also end up staying in darkness or living sinful lives like the people in the dream.

The dark mist surrounding the land was Satan, who tempts people and causes them to get lost and forget the path.

The large building filled with people represented the world who laugh at those trying to keep the commandments and be good. But in the end, it's the people who reach the tree that will be the happiest.

For Lehi, the dream was even more—it was a prophecy that Laman, Lemuel, and all their descendants would not follow the Lord's path and would be lost in the darkness. The prophecy would, eventually, come true.

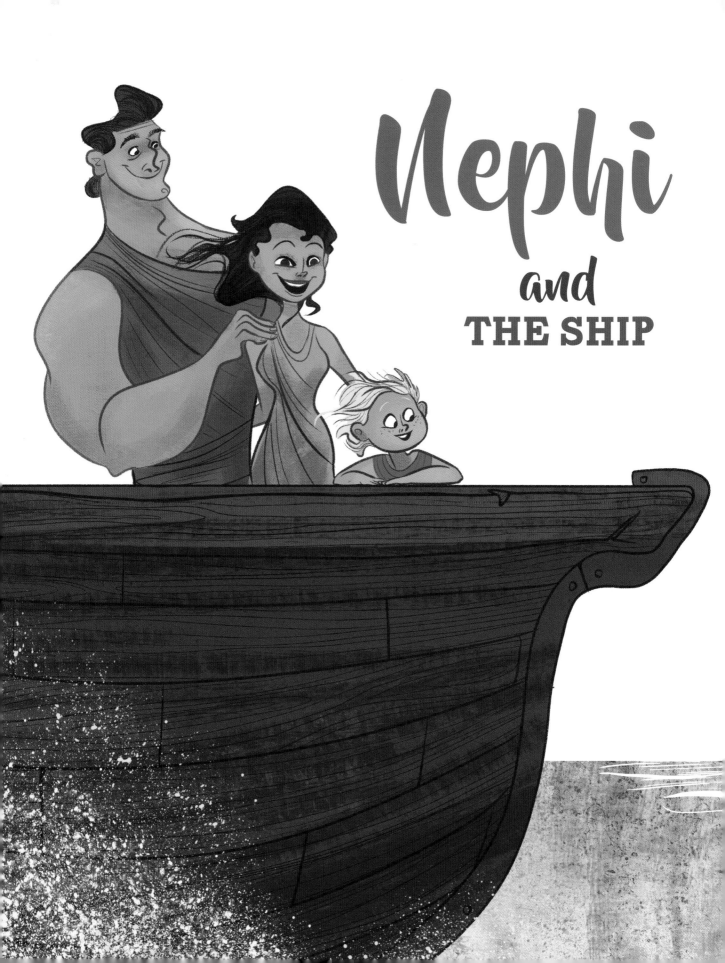

Nephi
and
THE SHIP

(1 NEPHI 17)

Lehi and his family traveled in the wilderness for eight years. They were often hungry, tired, and miserable, but their faith kept them going until they finally found a land near the sea that had everything they needed to be happy. They named the land Bountiful.

One day, Nephi was praying in the mountains, and the Lord revealed that Nephi and his family were going to cross the sea to the promised land in a ship that He would help them build.

Nephi was filled with faith and asked the Lord to show him where to find ore to make tools. When Lama and Lemuel heard about the ship, they laughed, doubtful that Nephi could even speak to the Lord.

Nephi reminded them of all the miracles the Lord had performed before like saving the children of Israel, parting the Red Sea, and giving them manna when they were hungry in the wilderness.

Laman and Lemuel were angry that their younger brother would try to teach them, and so they tried to hurt Nephi. Before they could even touch him, Nephi warned them that he was filled with the Spirit. As Nephi lifted his hands, the Lord gave Nephi power to shock his brothers. This miracle surprised Laman and Lemuel, who finally helped Nephi build the ship, knowing that he actually was guided by the Lord.

Nephi
and
THE PROMISED LAND

(1 NEPHI 18, 2 NEPHI 4–5)

Nephi loaded the finished ship with his family and all their belongings and then set sail for the promised land, following the direction of the Liahona.

After traveling for a while, Laman, Lemuel, and the sons of Ishmael became wicked. It was easy for them to forget the blessings the Lord had given them. Nephi warned his brothers to repent, but they were angry with his preaching and tied him up.

The ship was rocked with huge waves, and the Liahona stopped working. After four days of stormy seas, Laman and Lemuel finally understood that this was the power of the Lord and released Nephi. Immediately, Nephi prayed to the Lord. The water calmed, and they were back on course for the promised land.

The promised land was perfect, filled with everything they needed. Lehi's family was blessed for having so much faith and following the Lord's direction. They finally had a land to call their own.

When Lehi died, Nephi became the leader, which angered Laman and Lemuel. The Lord told Nephi to escape with those who were righteous. They built a new land, called Nephi, and called themselves the Nephites. The wicked who stayed behind were Lamanites.

Enos
and
HIS NEW FAITH

(ENOS 1)

Enos, Nephi's nephew, believed the teachings of God, but he hadn't kept the commandments. One day, while hunting, he was reminded of everything his father taught about God.

Enos prayed all day and into the night, until he heard a voice that said his sins had been forgiven.

The Lord explained that because of his faith, his sins had been erased. Feeling extremely happy, Enos prayed again, this time asking the Lord to bless all of the Nephites and the Lamanites.

With his new faith, Enos preached to all of the Nephites about the importance of keeping the commandments. The Nephites were sad that their relatives, the Lamanites, didn't know the power of God. The Nephites tried to teach the Lamanites, but they wouldn't listen because they had been taught by their fathers to hate the Nephites.

King Benjamin
and
HIS TEACHINGS

(MOSIAH 1–5)

The plates were handed down through generations until they reached a man named Benjamin, who was a good king and loved by his people. He protected his lands from the armies of the Lamanites, and there was peace. He always remembered to thank Heavenly Father and to keep the commandments.

When he reached old age, King Benjamin held a meeting to teach all of the Nephites everything he knew about the Lord. All the people in the land gathered to the temple, where they pitched their tents facing a tower where King Benjamin stood.

King Benjamin taught the Nephites that helping one another is the same as serving God. He begged them to keep all of the commandments, and he prophesied of the birth and death of Jesus Christ.

Continuing his speech, King Benjamin told everyone to believe in God's magnificent power, to be kind in how they spoke and acted, to teach their children to be righteous, and to love each other and not fight.

Once he had finished speaking, the Nephites fell on the ground and begged for forgiveness from God for their sins.

23

Zeniff and KING LAMAN

(MOSIAH 6, 9–10)

Mosiah, the son of King Benjamin, took over as king, ruling peacefully for years. Mosiah heard stories of a man named Zeniff, who went to live in the land of Nephi. Curious about what happened to them, Mosiah sent Ammon and other men to discover what happened to Zeniff.

Zeniff's story begins as a Nephite spy. He was sent by the ruler of the Nephites to find ways to destroy the Lamanites. After noticing that some Lamanites were good, Zeniff refused to complete his mission. He was sentenced to death for his disobedience, but his men fought back. Many soldiers died, but Zeniff escaped to Lehi-Nephi.

Once in Lehi-Nephi, Zeniff asked King Laman if he and his men could live in the land, King Laman agreed with the intention of stealing everything from Zeniff.

After thirteen years, King Laman's men began stealing Zeniff's crops and animals. Zeniff was faithful and skilled in battle—he knew what to do. He armed as many of his men as possible with swords, arrows, clubs, slings, and any other weapon they invented. Hearing the prayers of the people of Zeniff, the Lord helped them chase away the Lamanites, killing over three thousand of them in one day.

Abinadi and
HIS BRAVERY

(MOSIAH 11–17)

After King Zeniff died, his son Noah took over the land of Lehi-Nephi. Unlike his father, Noah was very selfish, sinful, and didn't care about the people of Lehi-Nephi.

Being greedy, he taxed his people one fifth of their food, crops, animals, gold, and silver. With the taxes he collected, he lived a lazy life, building extravagant buildings and homes for himself and his wicked friends.

When the Lamanites attacked Lehi-Nephi by sneakily killing people around the borders, King Noah sent just a few of his guards to defeat the Lamanites, but they were defeated. Noah then sent an army, which successfully fought off the Lamanites. King Noah was prideful and boasted of his success, although he had done very little.

Abinadi lived in Lehi-Nephi and was very faithful. He taught other people about the Lord and encouraged everyone to repent.

The people became angry because they didn't like being judged. Scared that he might be attacked, Abinadi wore a disguise and continued to teach in the city. One day, Abinadi was captured and brought to King Noah.

When Abinadi was brought before the king and his judges, he was not afraid. He told them all about the ten commandments and encouraged them to stop sinning. He warned that the Lord would destroy all the wicked people. King Noah refused to listen and commanded that Abinadi be killed, but the Lord protected him and no one could touch him until he had finished all of his teachings.

Before being taken away by the guards, Abinadi told King Noah that he, too, would die by fire—which eventually came true.

Alma
and
HIS ESCAPE

(MOSIAH 17–18)

Alma, one of King Noah's priests, heard everything Abinadi taught and knew he was a prophet from God. Because Alma begged King Noah not to kill Abinadi, Alma was also sentenced to death—so he ran into the wilderness to be safe.

Alma hid for days writing down Abinadi's teachings, which he used to secretly teach the Nephites about the Lord. Hundreds of people believed him and were baptized in a river called the Waters of Mormon.

Alma encouraged the people to build a strong faithful community, where they cared about and loved each other.

He taught them to share their possessions with the community so they could all thrive together.

Alma
and
HIS TEACHINGS

(MOSIAH 18–19)

Alma received power from God to ordain priests, who he trained to lead different churches. They met every week on the Sabbath day and worshipped the Lord together.

When King Noah found out about Alma, he sent guards to attack the camp, but Alma and his people were warned by the Lord and escaped into the wilderness. There were now four hundred people with Alma, and they referred to themselves as the Children of God.

Angry with King Noah, a man named Gideon tried to kill the king. He chased him to the top of a tower, where they saw the Lamanite army about to attack. King Noah convinced Gideon to let him live so that he could lead the armies to defeat the Lamanites.

King Noah lied, and instead forced his closest followers to run away with him, leaving their wives and children to be attacked by the Lamanites. Upset that their families may be in danger, King Noah's followers burned him to death. Abinadi's prophecy was fulfilled.

King Limhi
and
ZARAHEMLA

(MOSIAH 19–22)

King Limhi took over from his horrible father, Noah. Limhi cared about the people and worked hard to free them from the Lamanites, who had stolen their food, taken their possessions, and treated them like slaves.

By King Mosiah's command, Ammon and his brothers arrived in Lehi-Nephi to teach. When King Limhi learned they were sent from Zarahemla, he was happy, knowing how to help his people escape from the Lamanites.

Every night, the Lamanites would get very drunk. As part of his plan, Limhi sent extra wine to the borders of the city, knowing the Lamanites couldn't resist stealing the wine from the Nephites. When the guards were too drunk to protect the borders, all the Nephites safely escaped. They followed Ammon until they arrived safely in Zarahemla.

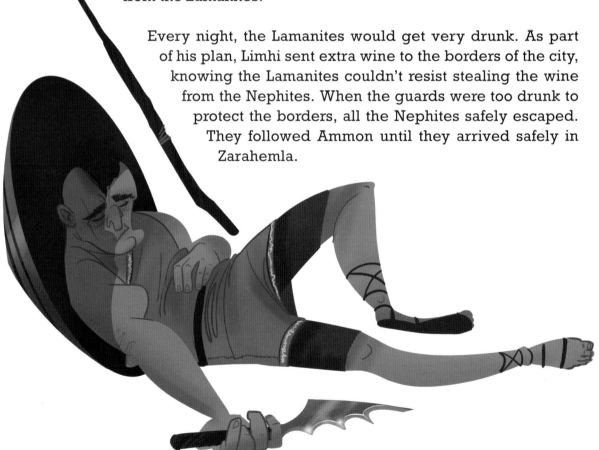

Alma
and the
SLEEPING GUARDS

(MOSIAH 24)

When the Lamanites realized that the Nephites had escaped, they followed King Limhi and his people into the wilderness, but they got lost. While wandering, they stumbled upon Alma and his people.

The people of Alma were afraid, but Alma reminded them to have faith. The Lamanites made the people of Alma their prisoners by surrounding them with guards and forcing them to hand over their food and possessions.

Alma told his people to stay faithful, because the Lord would keep them safe. One night the Lord caused the Lamanites to fall into a deep sleep. Knowing this was the Lord's plan, Alma gathered his people, and they slowly snuck away, finally escaping the imprisonment of the Lamanites.

The people of Alma were guided to the land of Zarahemla, where they were reunited with the Nephites and safe from the Lamanites.

Alma
and
ALMA THE YOUNGER

(MOSIAH 25–27)

When Alma arrived in Zarahemla, King Mosiah asked him to be the leader of the church.

Zarahemla had so many people living there that Alma couldn't teach everyone alone. He found trustworthy men and trained them to be leaders over smaller groups of people called congregations. They called themselves the Church of God.

Alma's son, Alma the Younger, didn't believe in the Church of God. He, like all the other children, hadn't heard the power of King Benjamin's sermon. Alma the Younger and others like him refused to go to church and be baptized.

Alma the Younger

and
THE SONS OF MOSIAH

(MOSIAH 27)

Alma the Younger did not listen and he did not believe his father. He tried to convince other people that the church was all a lie. Alma the Younger and the sons of King Mosiah wandered the city, laughing at the believers and convincing them to sin.

Over time, lots of people left the church because of how well Alma the Younger and his friends convinced them. They became a huge problem for the Church of God.

Alma the Younger
and
THE ANGEL

(MOSIAH 27)

One day, while spreading their lies and corruption, Alma the Younger and the sons of Mosiah were approached by an angel, who appeared in a cloud. The angel spoke like thunder, causing the earth to shake. Alma and his friends to fell to the ground.

The angel told them this was happening because so many righteous people had prayed to the Lord asking for Alma the Younger and his friends to stop destroying the church.

Alma the Younger was stunned and wasn't able to move or speak. The sons of Mosiah had to carry him home.

Alma was pleased when he heard what happened. He looked after his son, and gathered many church members to see the power of The Lord. The righteous members fasted and prayed asking the Lord to release Alma the Younger from his stupor.

After two days, Alma the Younger was freed. When he awoke, he told everyone about the pain and suffering he had felt in his soul. He knew the Lord was real, and after he had repented of his sins, the Lord had freed him.

Ammon
and
HIS MISSION

(MOSIAH 28–29, ALMA 17)

Alma the Younger and the sons of Mosiah made everything right by teaching the truth to those they had convinced to be wicked.

Mosiah's sons, Ammon, Aaron, Omner, and Himni, turned down their right to the throne and instead became missionaries, each traveling to different lands.

Having no one to take over as king, the people decide to elect judges, with Alma the Younger becoming the chief judge.

Ammon ventured to the land of Ishmael, where he was immediately tied up, and brought to King Lamoni. Alma explained that he wasn't a threat to them and that he just wanted to be one of the King's servants. King Lamoni agreed, and Ammon became one of the king's shepherds.

Ammon
and
KING LAMONI

(ALMA 17)

As Ammon and the servants were taking the flock to get water, some Lamanite thieves scattered the sheep. The other servants were terrified because the king had killed servants for losing his sheep before.

Ammon saw this as an opportunity to display the power of the Lord. Thinking quickly, he told the servants to gather the sheep. They were

successful, but while continuing their journey to the water, the Lamanites tried to scatter the sheep again.

Ammon told the servants to stay with the sheep while he fought the Lamanites using the power of the Lord. Using a sling, Ammon hurled rocks at the thieves. They fought back by attacking Ammon with clubs, but they were no match for a man with the Lord on his side. Ammon cut off their arms.

When the servants returned they told King Lamoni about Ammon's strength and showed him the dismembered arms as evidence.

Ammon
and
KING LAMONI'S FATHER

(ALMA 18–20)

King Lamoni wanted to hear about the power of the Lord. When he did, he felt the Spirit so strongly that he collapsed as if he were dead. When Lamoni finally woke up, he told everyone that he had seen a vision and knew that the Lord was real.

Lamoni insisted that Ammon teach his father, but the Lord prompted Ammon to go to the aid of his brother Aaron, who was imprisoned in the land of Middoni.

King Lamoni traveled with Ammon, and on their journey, they crossed paths with Lamoni's father. Shocked to see his son with a Nephite, he demanded that Lamoni kill Ammon. When Lamoni refused, his father tried to hurt him, but Ammon protected his friend, surprising King Lamoni's father with the strength of the Lord that Ammon possessed.

Finishing their journey to Middoni, Ammon freed his brother from prison, and in turn he traveled to teach King Lamoni's father about the gospel.

The People of Ammon and the END OF THEIR WEAPONS

(ALMA 23–24)

While Aamon, Aaron, Omner, and Himner taught in the Lamanite lands, the king decreed that they should be protected and that his people should listen to their teachings.

The Lamanites who were converted called themselves the Anti-Nephi-Lehies, or the people of Ammon.

There were many Lamanites who did not believe in the teachings of Christ. They were angry with the king and prepared for war. After the king died, his son named Anti-Nephi-Lehi ruled the Lamanites.

The king knew that the Lamanites were going to attack, so he spoke to his people, reminding them of how blessed they were to be counted among the Children of God. The people of Ammon, who had previously been a bloodthirsty people, didn't want to sin anymore, so instead of preparing for war, they buried their weapons deep in the ground and promised Heavenly Father that they would never fight again.

When they were attacked, the people of Ammon refused to take up their weapons and fight back. They prayed to the Lord, asking to be saved. Seeing that the people of Ammon wouldn't fight back, the Lamanites retreated after only killing a few of the people. Their faith and strength became an example that converted many of the Lamanites.

The next time the Lamanites attacked, they ran away to Zarahemla, where the Nephites welcomed them.

Korihor
and
HIS SIGN

(ALMA 30)

Korihor, a wicked man, traveled to Zarahemla, telling the people that there was no God. He claimed that everything they had been taught was a lie, that there would be no Messiah, and that there was nothing after death. He encouraged them to enjoy their life and not to worry about being righteous. Many people were easily convinced, but others knew Korihor was a liar and brought him to Alma, the chief judge.

Korihor asked Alma to prove the existence of God by performing a miracle. Alma explained that the testimonies of people and the scriptures were miracles themselves. Korihor laughed at Alma and denied the signs of God.

Alma warned that if Korihor would seek to tempt God and ignore the signs that had already been given, he would receive a sign but he wouldn't like it. Immediately Korihor tried to speak, but he couldn't. He had been struck dumb. He motioned to Alma that he believed, begging for the curse to be lifted. Alma, knowing that Korihor would lie again, said he could have his voice back when the Lord trusted him to use it for good.

Korihor never spoke again, and he eventually met a gruesome end by being trampled to death.

Alma and THE ZORAMITES

(ALMA 31–32)

The Zoramites believed in a God, but they did not know the truth. They were not committed to being righteous all the time, and they cared more for money. They used an altar called the Rameumpton to stand on and recite rehearsed prayers together.

Alma taught the Zoramites the truth, starting with the poorest because they weren't even allowed in the churches. The Zoramites that believed Alma went to live in Jershon with the people of Ammon.

Alma taught about faith, comparing it to a seed. He explained that both start very small, but when you care for a seed, it will grow, eventually producing delicious fruit. The same is true of faith. When you work at growing your faith, it will become great and magnificent and blessings will come.

Captain Moroni
and
HIS BRAVE ARMY

(ALMA 43–44)

Knowing that the leader of the Lamanites planned to attack Jershon, Alma asked Moroni, a mighty man who was only twenty-five but incredibly smart, to become the captain of the Nephite army.

Captain Moroni knew that the Nephites were outnumbered, so he had to make a plan. He made all the people in his army carry a shield, wear thick clothing, and dress in armor. This was the opposite of the Lamanites who wore nothing except a loincloth into battle. Seeing how prepared the Nephites were, the Lamanites ran away scared.

But Captain Moroni didn't just let them get away. He knew the Lamanites would come back, so he sent spies to their camp to find out what they were planning.

Discovering that Zerahemnah planned to attack Manti, a weaker city, Moroni took some of his army in secret and went to warn the people. He encouraged all the men in Manti to make weapons and prepare for war. He split the army into different groups, hiding them throughout the banks of a huge river called Sidon.

They jumped out and attacked the Lamanites as they travelled near the river. The Lamanites fought harder than ever before, inspired by techniques the Zoramites had taught them.

Captain Moroni's army began dying quickly, even though they had armor. Fighting for their freedom and defending their families, the Nephites found even more strength, crying to the Lord for help. They felt powerful again, and the Lamanites were afraid, most of them running away into the river, but there were more armies waiting for them. The Lamanites were trapped.

Captain Moroni approached Zerahemnah and explained that the Lord had helped them fight the Lamanites. Moroni demanded that the Lamanites drop all of their weapons, leave, and promise never to attack again. Zerahemnah refused, so Moroni declared that the battle would end when all of the Lamanites were destroyed.

Zerahemnah lunged at Moroni, but one brave Nephite jumped in the path, breaking Zerahemnah's sword and cutting the scalp of his head off. The soldier placed the scalp on the end of his sword, holding it up for all the Lamanites to see. He gave a warning that they would all die if they did not leave.

Many of the Lamanites ran away, but Zerahemnah just became more angry. With his remaining soldiers, he continued the battle until the Nephite army had slain almost all the of Lamanites. At that point, Zerahemnah surrendered and promised to stay peaceful.

Captain Moroni
and
THE TITLE OF LIBERTY

(ALMA 45–46)

Helaman, the son of Alma took the responsibility of the plates. Through all the wars, confusion about the church had become rampant, and a man named Amalickiah was taking advantage of the confusion, teaching the people to live without the church. He hoped to gain enough followers to take over and become king.

After seeing the sacrifices of the armies, Captain Moroni was angry. They had fought for their beliefs, and now the people were turning their back on the church. He ripped his coat and wrote: "In memory of our God, our religion, and freedom, and our peace, our wives, and our children."

He called it the title of liberty and hoisted it to the top of a pole, turning it into a flag. He dressed in his armor and prayed publicly for the safety of those who believed in Christ, begging the people to keep their religion and continue to be blessed.

When Moroni had gathered enough righteous people, he found Amalickiah and intended to put an end to his false teachings and sinful life.

Amalickiah was scared and ran away with some of his followers and joined the Lamanites.

Copies of the title of liberty were made and placed all around the land to remind everyone of their covenants and blessings.

Helaman

and the

TWO THOUSAND STRIPLING WARRIORS

(ALMA 47–53)

Amalickiah manipulated his way to becoming king of the Lamanites, getting what he had always wanted. Filled with power and hatred toward the Nephites, he began wars, taking over Nephite cities one by one.

After attacking Bountiful, a Nephite army led by Teancum tried to fight off the Lamanites. Teancum saw the strength of their army and thought that if their leader were killed, they would leave the cities alone. Teancum bravely snuck into the Lamanite camp at night and killed Amalickiah in his sleep. The Lamanites were immediately taken over by Ammoron, and the wars continued.

Seeing how many of their people had been killed, the people of Ammon, who had taken the oath to never fight again, wanted to help. Helaman refused to let them fight. He knew that breaking a promise to the Lord was far worse than death in battle.

Only the adults took the oath, which meant their children wouldn't be breaking a promise if they fought. Helaman assembled an army of two thousand young boys, who were honest and trustworthy and had all been raised believing in the Lord. They had no experience in battle, but they fought to keep their families free from the Lamanites. They had so much faith that they knew God would keep them safe.

Helaman trained the boys and prepared them for battle. He called them his sons, and they spoke to him with the same respect they showed their own fathers; they became known as the two thousand stripling warriors.

Helaman and the stripling warriors marched to Judea to give provisions to the armies. In Judea, the leader of the Nephites was called Antipus. After receiving their provisions, the Nephite armies were able to fight off some of the Lamanites, but a lot still stayed in Judea.

So Helaman and Antipus came up with a plan to get the Lamanites to leave Judea for good. They planned to have the stripling warriors march to Judea pretending to attack. But when the Lamanites came out to defend themselves, rather than fight, the stripling warriors would run, leading the Lamanites far from the city and to a place where Anitpus' army was waiting to ambush and destroy the Lamanites.

The plan started off well. The stripling warriors teased the Lamanites out of Judea and led them to where Anitpus was waiting. But then everything started to go wrong. When Antipus's army attacked, most of the Lamanites kept chasing the stripling warriors rather than fighting.

Improvising, the stripling warriors and Helaman ran for days and days, hoping that Antipus's army would catch up and defeat the Lamanites.

One day, the Lamanites finally stopped chasing them. They didn't know if Antipus had caught the Lamanites, or if they were trying to trick the stripling warriors into fighting.

Tired of running, the stripling warriors told Helaman that they had faith that the Lord would keep them safe in battle. They bravely ran back to fight the Lamanites, but they discovered Antipus's army already there. The Lamanites were close to winning the battle, but once the stripling warriors joined the fight, they had enough power to defeat the Lamanites.

When the battle was finally over, Helaman counted every boy, afraid that some of them may have died. To his surprise, they were all alive—wounded, but alive! Helaman immediately thanked the Lord for protecting them.

Captain Moroni
and
PAHORAN

(ALMA 59–62)

When Moroni heard of Helaman's success, he was motivated to take back the rest of the Lamanite filled lands. He wrote to the chief judge, Pahoran, asking for more supplies and men to win the war.

Thousands of people were killed while waiting for Pahoran to respond. Moroni was angry, assuming that Pahoran was just ignoring the needs of the people.

When Pahoran finally wrote back, he explained that he had to flee from Zarahemla because a group of men called the king-men threw him out of power replacing him with a king. Pahoran asked Moroni to join a new army that would destroy the king-men and give freedom back to the people.

Moroni was happy that Pahoran was still a good man. He quickly gathered some of his army and marched to Pahoran's aid while recruiting new members of the army as they traveled. Moroni destroyed the king-men, and Pahoran returned to power and immediately sent supplies to the Nephite armies.

With food and supplies the Nephites were able to chase the Lamanites until they were all trapped in one place and surrounded by all the different Nephite armies.

Feeling angry for the years spent fighting, suffering, and watching his friends die, Teancum tried to end the war by sneaking into the Lamanite's camp and killing their leader. However, while trying to escape, Teancum was captured and killed by the Lamanite guards.

The next day, Moroni chased the Lamanites until they were out of the Nephite lands, and the wars were finally over.

Hagoth and
HIS BOAT

(ALMA 63)

A few years later, a large group of Nephites became curious about the land to the north. They began an expedition to explore the land.

Hagoth was among that group of Nephites. He was an adventurous man, and wanted to travel even further through the Americas. He built a large ship and brought many Nephites with him on his travels.

The original boat returned, gathering even more Nephites to help them venture further. More boats were built and large droves of people embarked on new adventures to find new lands. It's a mystery what happened to them.

Nephi, Lehi,
and
THE FIRE

(HELAMAN 5)

Helaman, the leader of the young army, had two grandsons named Lehi and Nephi.

They choose to live righteously just like the original Lehi and Nephi. Wandering from land to land, they successfully brought many Nephites back to the church. Seeing the positive impact they were having, they also went to teach the Lamanites and baptized thousands of them.

Feeling like they could achieve anything, they made their way to the land of Nephi, but they were thrown into prison. Scared, they prayed to the Lord, knowing that their faith would keep them safe.

When the guards tried to kill them, hot flames burned around them, keeping the guards away while Lehi and Nephi sat untouched and safe.

Suddenly, an earthquake shook the land and a dark fog covered the Lamanites, causing them to be stuck. The voice of the Lord boomed from the sky, warning the Lamanites to stop harassing Lehi and Nephi.

The Lamanites didn't understand what was happening. Luckily, a Nephite who had become a Lamanite was able to explain that they were seeing the power of God. He explained that the only way to stop the earthquake and the fog was to repent.

The Lamanites obeyed. They prayed, begging the Lord for help. Huge pillars of fire shot up around them, and they were filled with the joy of the Holy Ghost.

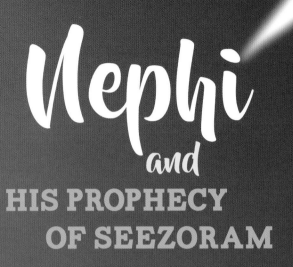

Nephi
and
HIS PROPHECY OF SEEZORAM

(HELAMAN 6–9)

Nephi returned home to Zarahemla, but the Gadianton robbers had corrupted the government and judges, who were making laws that didn't keep their people safe or righteous.

Nephi was shocked and disgusted at what had happened to his home. He prayed openly on a tower he built in his garden. He poured his soul into the prayer, gathering a crowd around him.

Nephi's prayer warned the crowd that if they continued sinning they would be destroyed. He told them the destruction had already begun because the chief judge, Seezoram, had been murdered by his brother.

Hearing the shocking news about Seezoram, five men ran to check. Just as Nephi had said, Seezoram was dead. Those five men knew that Nephi was telling the truth, they collapsed on the ground, afraid of the Lord because they finally understood how much they had sinned.

Some others came to check on Seezoram and assumed he had been murdered by the five men collapsed on the ground. They were tied up and imprisoned. Upon waking up, the five men tried to explain what had happened.

Rather than believe that Nephi was a prophet, the people decided Nephi had murdered Seezoram to trick them. Nephi knew who the

real murderer was and revealed his identity as Seantum, the brother of Seezoram. He said to send someone to Seantum's house and look for blood on his coat. After finding the blood, Seantum would confess.

When everything happened the way Nephi had prophesied, they knew he spoke with the power of God.

Nephi

and

THE FAMINE

(HELAMAN 10–11)

While praying, Nephi discovered the Lord's plan to destroy the wicked Nephites through war. Nephi loved all of the Nephites and tried to warn them that they would be killed. Rather than listen, the people put Nephi in prison.

Nephi escaped from prison and asked the Lord to change His plan and instead bring a famine to the land so that the Nephites might remember the blessings of the Lord.

The famine came, and thousands of people died because they wouldn't repent or remember the Lord.

When the famine was at its worst, the Nephites finally began to remember the Lord and the blessings He could bring. They repented and believed again. The people went to Nephi, knowing he could speak to the Lord. They asked Nephi to pray for them to be saved, for the famine to end.

Seeing the goodness that had returned to the Nephites, Nephi begged and prayed to the Lord to end the famine. Knowing they had repented, the Lord ended the famine, and the food returned to the Nephite lands. The Nephites were baptized and flourished happily for many years.

Gadianton
ROBBERS

(HELAMAN 11)

A group of evil people, calling themselves the Gadianton robbers, slowly convinced people to join them. Hiding in the wilderness in mountains and caves, they would come out at night to steal, murder, and commit horrible crimes in the cities and towns. They did all of these terrible things to get money and power. They were very sneaky and difficult to catch. Over time, they corrupted more and more people until eventually the Nephites were more wicked than the Lamanites.

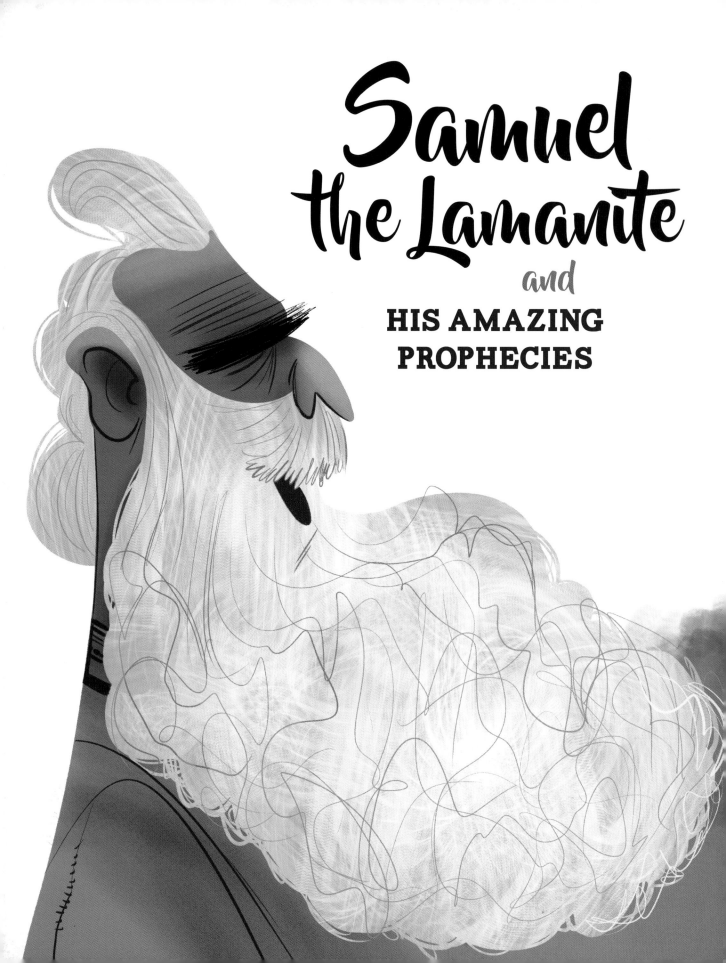

(HELAMAN 13)

About six years before Jesus was born, Samuel, who was a Lamanite, arrived in Zarahemla to teach the wicked Nephites about the Lord. He gave them a chance to repent of their sins and warned that they would be punished if they refused.

Samuel taught for days and days, but no one would listen to him. The Nephites became sick of being judged by Samuel, so they decided to throw him out of Zarahemla.

Samuel felt defeated and was upset that he wasn't able to save the Nephites, but fearing that he may be killed, he decided to go home.

Samuel the Lamanite and THE WALL

(HELAMAN 13–16)

As he was about to go home, Samuel was stopped by the Lord and told to return to Zarahemla. He was scared to go back, and when he arrived, they wouldn't let him back into the city. Refusing to disobey the Lord, Samuel climbed the wall of the city, and from there he taught the people. He prophesied that Jesus would be born soon. Samuel told them that on the night the Savior was born, the sky would stay bright all night, and a new star would appear in the sky.

He then told them about the death of Christ and how there would be three terrifying days of darkness, earthquakes, thunder, and lightning.

Samuel warned the Nephites that if they didn't repent now, then there was no guarantee that they would live when the Lord came.

Some Nephites believed Samuel. They ran to Nephi, knowing he still believed in God, and asked him to teach and baptize them. Most of the Nephites hated Samuel and wanted to kill him. They threw rocks and shot arrows at him, trying to make him fall off the wall.

Although hundreds of rocks and arrows were aimed at Samuel, none of them hit him. He was protected by the hand of the Lord. Seeing how incredible this was, more Nephites ran to be baptized.

Growing tired of the trickery and judgment, the wicked Nephites found the army captains and asked them to capture and imprison Samuel.

Knowing that his time was up, Samuel climbed down the wall and escaped from Zarahemla without being hurt.

The Nephites and the
SIGNS OF CHRIST'S BIRTH

(3 NEPHI 1)

Nephi left Zarahemla after passing the records down to his oldest son, who was also named Nephi. Over a few years, Nephi could see the wondrous signs and miracles that signaled the birth of the Lord was close.

Every night, those who believed waited for the sky to stay bright, and those who didn't believe laughed at the believers, telling them it was all lies.

The nonbelievers agreed that if the sign had not happened before a certain date, then all the believers would be murdered.

Hearing the plan to kill his people, Nephi prayed, begging the Lord for help. He received a strong revelation that that night was the night. And just as the prophecies had said, the sky didn't turn dark, and a new star appeared in the sky. Everyone knew this meant the Savior had been born.

Most of the nonbelievers were terrified. They were disappointed in themselves for how they had treated the believers. Now knowing that the Lord had been born, they repented and were baptized.

The *Nephites* and the
SIGNS OF CHRIST'S DEATH

(3 NEPHI 6–10)

The Nephites were blessed when they remembered the Lord their God, but the more blessings they received, they more they wanted. This made them greedy, prideful, slow to remember the Lord, and, eventually, sinful.

The judges became evil, abusing their power and killing the prophets. Trying to stop them was useless because they used secret combinations to escape any kind of punishment or imprisonment.

Soon, the land was filled with inequality, churches were based on how much money you had, and eventually, the government was destroyed with wickedness, splitting the Nephites into tribes.

One day, a storm arrived in the land, there was loud thunder, frightening lightning, earthquakes, and violent winds. Zarahemla was burned in fires, the city of Moroni was covered by large waves, and the city of Moronihah was destroyed when a mountain split the ground beneath it.

Then there was just darkness. Candles and fires wouldn't light, and the sun, moon, and stars didn't shine. The darkness lasted for three days, and during that time, the people cried and prayed, regretting their sins.

From the darkness, everyone heard a voice explaining that the people who were the worst sinners, who had murdered prophets, and tried to destroy the earth, were now dead—having been killed with the earthquakes, winds, and fires.

The voice continued, asking the remaining people if they were ready to finally repent of their sins and return to the ways of the Lord. The voice confirmed that Christ had died for the sins of the world and that the law of Moses was fulfilled.

The voice stopped, but everyone stayed quiet, no longer crying or complaining about the darkness.

After a few hours, the voice spoke again. This time, it reminded everyone of the blessings the Lord had given them, but chastised them for choosing to sin rather than have faith. This was now their chance to repent and be blessed again.

The darkness lasted for three days, then finally, light! The morning came, the earth stopped shaking, the winds stopped lashing, and the thunder grew silent.

The people were thrilled to be alive and grateful that they had a chance to repent.

Jesus Christ
and
HIS VISIT TO AMERICA

(3 NEPHI 11–16)

Finally the people talked again, confused about what they had just witnessed. They were stopped suddenly when another voice came from the sky, "This is my Beloved Son, who I am very proud of," the voice boomed. "Listen to Him."

A man, dressed in white robes, floated from the sky—He looked like an angel. Once the man was on the ground, He showed His hands and feet and the people saw the holes in them where He had been nailed to the cross.

The people knew it was Jesus Christ, and they fell to their knees with joy, praising and worshiping Him.

Just like in Jerusalem, Jesus selected twelve men to be His disciples. Among those twelve men was Nephi. Jesus gave the disciples the power of the priesthood so that they could baptize people into the church.

Jesus then turned to the people and told them they had to repent of their sins so they could be baptized—they could no longer steal, cheat, lie, boast, swear, take His name in vain, or fight. He told them that they had to be good members of His church, which involved loving everyone, even if they looked or talked differently and liked to do different things. He told them that they should no longer talk negatively about other people, judge them, or hurt them.

Jesus Christ
and
HIS BLESSING FOR THE CHILDREN

(3 NEPHI 17)

After teaching all day, Jesus told everyone to go home, rest, and pray for strength so they could learn even more in the morning. The people refused to go home—they didn't want to be away from Jesus because He was so wonderful to be around. Jesus felt so much love for them that He agreed to stay longer and perform miracles by healing everyone who was sick.

Once all the sick and injured people were healed, Jesus asked for all the children to come gather around Him. He began praying for and blessing the children. The prayer was so beautiful, real, and compassionate. Once He finished praying, the sky opened up and angels poured out of the sky, ministering to every child and blessing each one.

It was an incredible thing to see, a true miracle. The people watched filled with surprise and happiness and were grateful to be in the presence of the Lord.

Jesus Christ
and the
SACRAMENT PRAYER

(3 NEPHI 18)

After blessing the children, Jesus asked the twelve disciples to bring bread and water so He could teach the people about the sacrament.

Jesus broke the bread into small pieces,while telling the people that they should take the sacrament every week. The bread was to symbolize His body, which He had freely given so that all could live again after death. The water was to symbolize the blood He willingly shed in the Garden of Gethsemane when He took upon Himself everyone's sins so that all can repent and be clean again.

Jesus promised that if the people were good enough to take the sacrament and kept their promises to Heavenly Father, they would always have the Holy Ghost with them.

Jesus Christ
and the
UNBELIEVABLE PRAYER

(3 NEPHI 19)

The twelve disciples became missionaries by splitting into small groups to teach people about prayer and repentance—after each person repented, the disciples baptized them with the power that had been given to them by Jesus. With that power, they were able to perform miracles, and ordinances in Jesus's name.

Seeing how righteous the people in the Americas had become, Jesus started praying to Heavenly Father, asking for the Holy Ghost to always be with the people. Jesus continued praying, saying the most wonderful, unbelievable things—the people, even Nephi, were so impressed and excited by Jesus's prayer that they felt incredibly happy.

Jesus Christ
and His
INCREDIBLE DISCIPLES

(3 NEPHI 28)

Before leaving the earth to be with His Father, Jesus asked His disciples what they wanted the most. Nine of the disciples asked to live with Jesus after their missions on earth were complete.

Jesus promised that at the age of seventy-two, the nine disciples would be brought to heaven to live a wondrous eternity with Him.

The other three disciples wanted to stay on earth teaching people for as long as they could. It seemed like a big thing to ask for, so they were scared to ask Jesus.

Jesus could hear their desires in their hearts and told them they could receive this righteous desire. They would stay on earth until Jesus returned again at the Second Coming. They became known as the Three Nephites.

Over hundreds of years, the Three Nephites would wander from country to country, helping people and teaching them about the gospel. They'd be thrown in prison, burned, and attacked by animals, but they would still live, preaching the gospel and preparing the world for when Christ would visit again.

Happy with having their desires fulfilled, the twelve disciples sadly said goodbye to Jesus before He left earth, ascending back to Heaven to be with Heavenly Father.

America
and PEACE

(4 NEPHI 1)

The disciples wanted to share everything Jesus had taught them. They traveled to all the different cities in the country, telling people the truth and giving their powerful testimony of the Lord. Because they had been given the priesthood, they were able to baptize thousands of people, form churches, and teach members about taking the sacrament weekly to remember the sacrifices of Jesus.

The disciples had the authority to perform miracles, like healing sick people and giving blind people their sight. On a few occasions, they even brought people back from the dead.

The happiness that Jesus had brought with Him spread through the land, it was a peaceful, wonderful time to be alive.

After two hundred years passed, Amos, the grandson of Nephi, took over the responsibility of writing the plates. There was no one left on earth who had met Jesus and remembered what it was like to be in His presence and feel His Spirit, so it became difficult for the people to believe in the gospel. Some people became greedy, wanting more money, nice clothes, and lots of expensive possessions.

This greed caused disagreements, which led to the formation of different churches that split up the rich people from the poor. Secret combinations crept back into the land.

Each church changed the scriptures and commandments so that they could do sinful things and still look like they were religious. This wickedness grew for thirty years until each group was big enough to build their own communities again: the Nephites, Jacobites, Josephites, and Zoramites still believed in the Lord, but the Lamanites, Lemuelites and Ishmaelites lived by their own beliefs.

The Lamanites, Lemuelites, and Ishmaelites taught their children to hate those who believed in Christ. Over the next three hundred years, the number of nonbelievers grew until the only people left who believed in Christ were the Three Nephites who had asked to stay on earth forever.

Mormon
and
THE GOLD PLATES

(MORMON 1–10)

At the age of ten, a boy named Mormon was given the responsibility of continuing the record of the people. He was told where the plates were hidden and asked to watch and remember everything that happened to the people. When he was twenty-four, he retrieved the plates and wrote everything he remembered. He also started rewriting all of the plates into one record engraved on gold plates.

Living in Zarahemla, he wrote about all the tragic wars that had happened between the Nephites and the Lamanites. He became the leader of the Nephite armies. Because he was big and strong, he was perfect for the job.

Mormon taught his armies about Jesus Christ. He asked them to repent and have faith because if they were righteous, the Lord would protect them in battle. The Nephites wouldn't listen to Mormon, and most of them died because they wouldn't be worthy of and ask for the Lord's help.

With so many Nephites dying, Mormon knew that the Nephites were going to lose the war. He gave the gold plates to his son, Moroni, with strict instructions on how to finish the writing.

Mormon put on his armor and led his army into battle one last time. Knowing that the gold plates and the history of the Nephites were safe, he bravely fought the Lamanites. Because the Nephites never called on God for help, every single one of them was killed, including Mormon. The only Nephite left alive was Moroni, who was left alone with the plates.

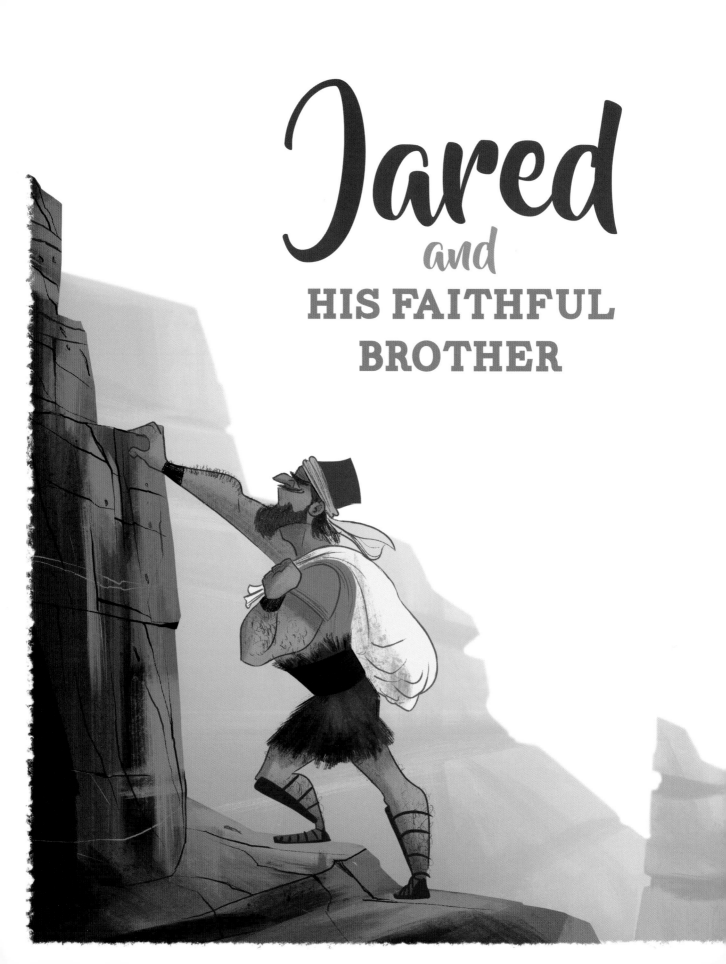

Jared
and
HIS FAITHFUL
BROTHER

(ETHER 1)

While Mormon worked on condensing all of the records, he uncovered the records of an ancient, lost civilization who left their homeland and traveled to the Americas hundreds of years before Lehi and Nephi. These people were called the Jaredites.

Jared and his family, called the Jaredites, lived in Babel. The people in Babel wanted to meet God, so they built a tower so tall that they believed it would touch heaven to find Him. God was angry with their pride, and He punished the wicked people in Babel by giving them all different languages so they could no longer speak the same language.

Jared and his family had been righteous, so their family could still understand each other. Jared was scared of God's anger and asked his brother to pray to find out what they should do. Their answer was to leave Babel as soon as possible.

They were told to gather their family, their belongings, lots of food, many different seeds, and a male and female of all their animals. The Lord promised to guide them to an incredible land, a promised land filled with food and water.

The Brother of Jared and THE BARGES

(ETHER 2)

The Lord guided the Jaredites through the wilderness to the seashore. The Jaredites set up their camp and had everything they needed. They lived there happily for four years.

Suddenly, the Lord appeared to the brother of Jared in a fierce cloud. He was angry with the brother of Jared because he'd forgotten his faith and had sinned. He had stopped at the seashore instead of continuing on to the promised land, ignoring the Lord's direction.

The brother of Jared repented immediately and asked for forgiveness from the Lord. The Lord said He would forgive the brother of Jared, but He warned him not to sin anymore. He warned the brother of Jared that the Spirit would not always be with him and that if he continued to ignore the Lord, he would be cut off from the presence of God.

The Lord told the brother of Jared that he and his family were to cross the sea. If the brother of Jared followed the Lord's directions perfectly, then they would be able to build barges to cross the sea in safety.

With the Lord's guidance, the Jaredites built eight small barges that were completely watertight and floated on top of the water.

The *Brother of Jared* and THE GLOWING STONES

(ETHER 2–3)

The brother of Jared was worried about the barges because there was no way to get light, no way to get air, and no way to steer the barges.

The Lord gave the brother of Jared the instructions to make air holes by drilling holes in each barge and blocking them with a stopper. When they needed air, they could unstop the hole, let air in, and plug the hole again when water started to splash in.

The holes only solved one of the problems, so the brother of Jared asked the Lord again about the darkness of the barges. The Lord told the brother of Jared that windows or fire would cause the barges to sink. The brother of Jared knew the Lord was right, so he thought for a few minutes and came up with a creative solution. He asked the Lord if He would touch a set of stones so they would shine brightly and light the barges inside.

The Lord was impressed with the brother of Jared's faith, so He reached out His finger and touched each of the stones. Because of his great faith, the veil was removed from the brother of Jared, and he saw the Lord's finger. The brother of Jared was surprised that it looked just like his.

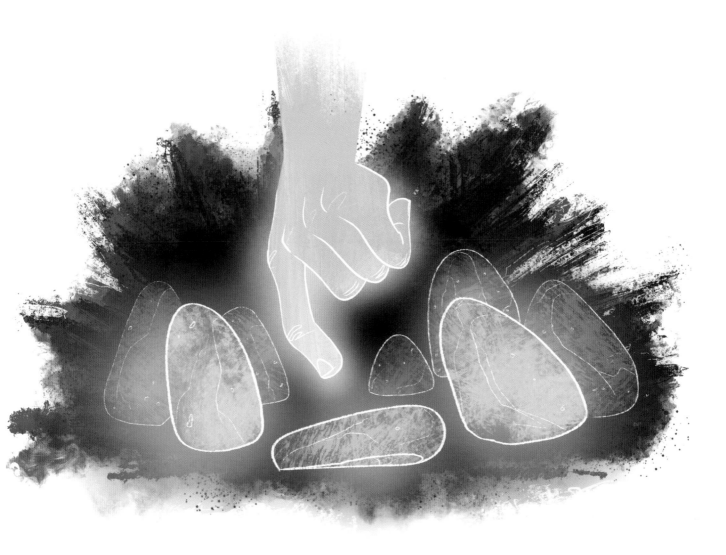

Curious about what the Lord looked like, the brother of Jared felt brave and asked the Lord if He would show Himself. Because of his faith, the Lord revealed Himself and taught the brother of Jared many things about the gospel.

The brother of Jared thanked the Lord for all of the blessings he'd given the Jaredites. Then when they were ready, the Jaredites loaded everything onto their barges and sealed themselves in. They floated on the water while the Lord guided them.

The Jaredites lived inside the barges for almost a year until they finally arrived in a new land.

The Jaredites and THEIR DESTRUCTION

(ETHER 6–15)

The Jaredites were very thankful to the Lord for bringing them to a land filled with all the food they needed. They lived there happily for a long time. One of Jared's sons became the king of Jaredites before Jared and his brother died.

For many years they were happy. The Jaredites were righteous and thankful, and the Lord blessed them—until a man named Corihor would bring about the destruction of the Jaredites.

It started small. Corihor didn't want to follow the commandments of the Lord. He lost his faith, and he refused to listen to the teachings of the Church. Seeing his example, others started to follow. Groups of people became wicked and rejected the Lord. They formed their own communities, and when they disagreed with one another, wars and battles began.

The Lord wanted to save the Jaredites, so He chose a man named Ether to become a prophet. Ether's mission was to remind the wicked Jaredites about how the Lord had blessed them and saved them from destruction. No one would listen to Ether, and instead, the wicked Jaredites tried to kill him.

Ether, scared for his life, ran away and hid in some caves. He stayed in the caves during the day, and at night, he would sneak into the towns to teach people. When Ether's mission seemed to be failing, the Lord sent Ether to talk to the king, but he wouldn't listen either. Feeling the Spirit running through him, Ether prophesied that if the king didn't listen, then he would live to witness the end of the Jaredites.

The king still didn't listen, so the Lord cursed the land with an extraordinary punishment. Every time a wicked Jaredite left a weapon or tool on the ground, it would vanish into the earth. This caused a lot of confusion and fear. Even seeing this miracle still didn't convince the Jaredites to repent. The wars continued, and slowly everyone was killed except for the king, who watched as the Jaredites were completely wiped out—just as Ether had warned.

Moroni and

THE GOLD PLATES

(MORONI 1–9)

Once Mormon died, Moroni was all alone. He finished writing the gold plates while keeping them safe from the dangerous Lamanites. He was grateful every day to be alive so he could finish his father's work.

When he had finished condensing all the plates into one set, Moroni wrote some of the revelations he had received from Heavenly Father, including the prayers that Jesus used to ordain His disciples as priests and bless the Sacrament.

Moroni wrote about how important it is for us to repent of our sins and be baptized. It's also important for us to go to church every week, to be around people who believe the same things as us, and to look after each other. Going to church every week helps us confirm that we're making good decisions and that we're on the path back to Heavenly Father.

Moroni understood that life today would be hard. He knew that there would be difficult things all of us would have to face. But he reminded us of Christ's promise that if we have faith, we will have the power to overcome the things that seem too hard for us to achieve.

Moroni and
THE WONDERFUL PROMISE

(MORONI 10)

Moroni finished the gold plates by making a promise that if you read the scriptures seriously, think about them, have faith in Christ, and want to know the truth—then ask Heavenly Father through a prayer and the Holy Ghost will tell you everything is true.

Moroni also taught that the Lord is responsible for all the blessings in our lives and that we should thank Him every single day for our experiences and blessings.

The Holy Ghost has a very important job: He can confirm the truth, He helps guide us to make good choices, and He can warn us of danger. He's always there to guide us through life when we're following the commandments. By making us feel warm and happy, He confirms that we're making good choices. And by making us feel uneasy, He's warning us when we are making choices that will lead us off the path.

By using the Holy Ghost, people can do different things: some people will be able to speak different languages, others will be able to see angels, some people will perform miracles, and others may be able to heal sicknesses. There are so many things, Moroni taught, that we can do with faith in Christ, and the Holy Ghost will help us achieve these amazing things.

Moroni
and
HIS JOURNEY TO THE END

(MORMON 8, MORONI 10)

The Lamanites had taken over the whole land and murdered anyone who believed in Christ. Moroni refused to deny his faith, so he hid and wandered from city to city, living in the wilderness. He escaped being captured for years.

Moroni was the last faithful Nephite. He didn't want the truth to be lost, so he finished writing the gold plates and then, under direction from the Lord, buried them in the Hill Cumorah, so no one would accidentally find them. He then wandered the land, trying to stay alive, and did his best to live a righteous life in a wicked land.

Joseph Smith
and
HIS HUNT FOR THE TRUTH

(JOSEPH SMITH—HISTORY 1)

Joseph Smith was born two days before Christmas in 1805. His family traveled a lot when he was young, and when he was fourteen, he lived in Manchester, New York. It was a very confusing time because there were lots of churches and they all taught different things based on the Bible. Every church claimed that they knew the way back to Heavenly Father and accused every other church of being wrong.

Joseph loved learning about all the religions. He went to all of the different churches to listen to their teachings and discover which one was true. Most of Joseph's family were Presbyterian, but Joseph didn't think it was the true church.

One night, Joseph was reading his Bible, fascinated by the stories and teachings. He read a verse that would change his life forever. The verse was James 1:5, which told him that if he had a question, then he just had to ask God, and if he had enough faith, he'd be given the answer.

Joseph Smith and His

LIFE-CHANGING PRAYER

(JOSEPH SMITH—HISTORY 1)

Ready to find out the truth, Joseph Smith went to the forest near his house. When he started to pray, he felt a strong, dark, powerful force stopping him. The mysterious power stopped him from moving and forced his mouth shut so he couldn't speak. Joseph was terrified. The darkness was so powerful, he was afraid that it would kill him.

Finding the strength to cry out, Joseph asked God to help him be free from the evil holding him. As soon as he prayed to God, the evil force was gone. Suddenly, there was brightness all around him and a beam of light that was brighter than the sun appeared above him. From the light, Heavenly Father and Jesus Christ appeared to Joseph. Heavenly Father called to Joseph

by name, then pointed to Jesus and said, "This is my Beloved Son. Hear Him!"

Joseph was shocked at what was happening. He was seeing God and Jesus! He remembered his questions, and he quickly asked which church he should join. To Joseph's surprise, Jesus told him that no religion on earth had the full teachings. Joseph was then given instructions and told that he was to bring about the restoration of the one true church to the earth.

After praying, Joseph told many people about seeing God and Jesus. But instead of being happy and curious, they were angry and told him he had been tricked by the devil.

But Joseph knew what he had felt. He knew that what he had seen and heard was real. And he could not deny it.

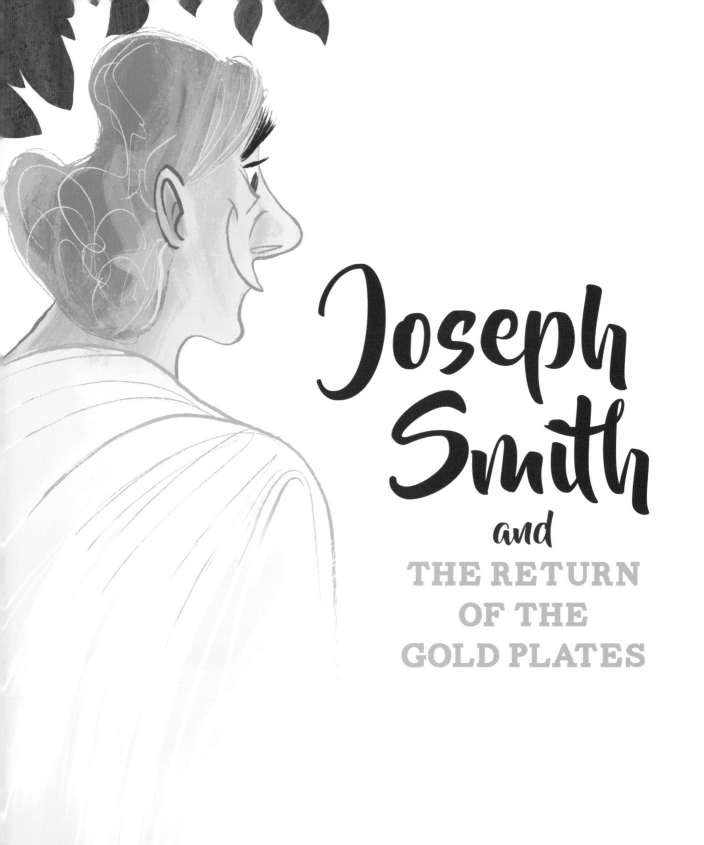

Joseph Smith

and

THE RETURN OF THE GOLD PLATES

(JOSEPH SMITH—HISTORY 1)

Every night that Joseph prayed he hoped to learn more about the true church, and one night it happened—Moroni appeared to Joseph as an angel. He told Joseph about a record that was buried nearby and that contained the true teachings of God. Moroni told Joseph that in a few years, he would translate the plates with help from stones that were also buried with them.

Moroni disappeared, and Joseph went to bed stunned by what he had learned. Then Moroni appeared two more times, saying the exact same thing word for word to make sure Joseph understood everything.

After waiting excitedly for four years, the day finally came that Joseph could dig up the plates. Moroni showed him exactly where they were and warned him not to show them to anyone.

Joseph had a lot of people trying to steal the plates from him, but thankfully the power of God made sure they stayed safe with Joseph until after the translation was finished.

Joseph Smith

and

THE BOOK OF MORMON

(JOSEPH SMITH—HISTORY 1)

Joseph and his friend Oliver Cowdery began the difficult task of translating the plates. Using the seer stones, Joseph read aloud the fascinating stories from the plates, and Oliver wrote everything down.

While reading, Oliver and Joseph became curious about baptism, so they prayed together to find out more. John the Baptist appeared and gave Joseph and Oliver the Aaronic Priesthood. They immediately baptized each other, becoming the very first members of The Church of Jesus Christ of Latter-day Saints.

While finishing the translation, Oliver and Joseph were attacked many times, some translated pages were stolen, and people called them liars, but they kept working hard and eventually they finished the translation and printed the Book of Mormon.

A lot of wicked people wanted to destroy the church, so they attacked Joseph. Bringing the truth back to the earth was a very difficult thing, but because of his faith, Joseph succeeded. Without Joseph's faith and sacrifices, we would not have the true church on the earth today.

Conclusion

The stories you have just read are more than just stories—they are lessons to remember through our lives. We can learn from the stories of the faithful and the unfaithful because we know what happens when we are disobedient, and we can also see the happiness that comes from Heavenly Father when we keep the commandments.

By praying every day, we will give Heavenly Father the chance to bring the stories from the Book of Mormon to our minds when we need to remember them. Then we can use those stories to make good decisions that keep us on the straight and narrow path from Lehi's dream. We can remember the love Nephi had for his brothers and love our friends and families the same way. We can choose to have faith like the brother of Jared and teach people about the gospel like Alma the Younger.

Being given this special record at this time is Heavenly Father's way of helping us make difficult choices in a very complicated world, making good decisions all the time is hard, but reading the stories of the Book of Mormon often will help us all to lead a happy righteous life.